# WEST COAST BUNG/
## OF THE 1920s

### With Photographs and Floor Plans

A Street *of* South Pasadena Bungalows

# E. W. STILLWELL & COMPANY

## Dover Publications, Inc., Mineola, New York

IT SEEMS quite natural for a good many Eastern clients to ask (because we are in California) if Stillwell houses will be substantial in a severe climate. If customary precautions are taken against extreme cold, such bugaboos will disappear.

". . . I have become thoroughly convinced that the Bungalow is **just as practical in a cold climate** as it is in a warmer climate. I built mine to stand the winter and the test that we have recently had (record winter of 1912-13) **proves conclusively that they are as warm and as comfortable as any house** possibly can be. Every one of the occupants of my houses keep all inside doors open and the furnaces keep the houses as **warm as a summer's day.** . . . The test I have given the houses should be of some value to you in selling the plans, especially for our climate. They are all built from your plans.

"If there are any of these views you care to use, you are at liberty to do so. The trees were covered with ice, as you will notice, at the time pictures were taken, so you have a typical Bungalow shown in midwinter."

S. F. LLOYD.

Edwardsville, Illinois.

EIGHT ILLINOIS (STILLWELL-CALIFORNIA) BUNGALOWS WARM AS A SUMMER'S DAY

*Bibliographical Note*

This Dover edition, first published in 2006, is an unabridged republication of the work originally published by E. W. Stillwell & Co., Los Angeles, California, in 1919 under the title *West Coast Bungalows.*

*Library of Congress Cataloging-in-Publication Data*

West Coast bungalows.
  West Coast bungalows of the 1920s : with photographs and floor plans / E.W. Stillwell & Company.
    p. cm.
  Originally published: West Coast bungalows. Los Angeles, Calif. : E.W. Stillwell & Co., 1919.
  ISBN 0-486-44718-9 (pbk.)
    1. Bungalows—California—Designs and plans. I. E.W. Stillwell & Co. II. Title.
NA7571.W47 2006
728'.3730222794—dc22

2006042335

Manufactured in the United States of America
Dover Publications, Inc., 31 East 2nd Street, Mineola, N.Y. 11501

# A Personal Talk About the Stillwell Service

IN CALIFORNIA we have new ways of doing things that seem to interest people everywhere. Los Angeles is literally the melting-pot of the Nation, people coming here from every State — and from every corner of the earth. Thousands come annually for the sole purpose of making homes.

We have a fortunate combination of circumstances. The money-means is at hand — every kind of building material — a high class of permanent residents — a constant influx of newcomers who appreciate the best — with artists, architects, designers and homebuilders in the greatest rivalry for the favor of the public.

California homes cover an amazing range of style and cost. Home-planning and home-building are fine arts. It is well within the truth to say that in this respect this city is fully twenty-five years ahead of any other. Southern California Homes are models for all the world.

You can put the spirit and style of California in your home, no matter where you build; you will always be glad of it. But for best results and economy in building, you must be careful to get plans from specialists in house planning. The average builder is wholly unqualified to build a 100 per cent successful home from a picture and floor plan only. There are few planning agencies competent and experienced enough to render satisfactory service by correspondence.

We have tried to make our plan books truly representative of the latest developments in California homebuilding — to show the greatest possible variety and range of styles. To do this we have combed the country for the very best designs and have increased the variety of our offerings by including some of these with our own. *For those designs not originated by us we have made new and, we believe, better interior floor plans.* Exteriors have been carefully kept in complete conformity with the illustrations. Our plans enable any builder anywhere faithfully and economically to reproduce any house without supervision.

The room arrangement and the character of construction of most California houses would make them quite unsuited for other climatic conditions. Also the original plans and specifications from which they are built cannot often be used with any satisfaction elsewhere. But the style — the architecture, like clothes fashions — can be adapted to varying conditions.

I believe that we know the real needs of the home-builder in almost every locality. I was a resident of South Dakota for twenty-five years, and know what extremes of heat and cold are, wind, sun, snow and rain. Nearly every person employed here has had similar experience. We know the necessities of your climate, and that the plans we offer are adaptable to your needs no matter where you live.

Our work is so arranged that I can give personal direction to most of the inquiries which come in. When you deal with us, I want you to feel that you are dealing with some one who will treat your problems as an individual responsibility. Our success is based on this foundation of real service.

The idea of publishing these California designs with improved working plans so that people everywhere may have better and more attractive homes, has always appealed to the writer and his associates so strongly that it has been made a life work. The books have been compiled right here in our own office and I do not think any statement is exaggerated. They are not the exuberant claims of paid advertising agents, written merely to get your money, but rather to help you secure the most value for your investment when you build.

This business was begun in 1906 and taken over under the present name in 1907. Thousands of houses have been built from our plans since that time, most of which were secured through our correspondence system. We have studied the building question from the standpoint of the needs of our clients not only in every part of the United States, but in foreign countries as well.

Note that all published Stillwell plans are guaranteed to be satisfactory, as represented. We are willing to send plans on approval (according to any of the several offers on page 57) so that you can inspect them, compare them with any others, or have them figured by your contractor.

Why not take advantage of this proposition?

*E. W. Stillwell*

# Age of the Bungalow

ETHEL BROOKS STILLWELL
(With Apologies to Kipling)

¶ When Earth's last House has been banished,
And the era of Homes has come in,
When the last of the building is finished,
And the hammers have ceased their din,
We shall rest—and, faith, we shall need it—
Content for a century through,
Till the Master of all good builders
Shall set us to work anew.

¶ Then they that have homes shall be happy,
They shall sit in their bungalows
From the fiercest heat of the tropics
To the deepest of arctic snows.
They shall know real comfort in living
And freedom from Custom's thrall,
And the work of the homes shall be lightened;
It shall hardly be work at all.

¶ There shall be no towers to vex us,
No meaningless gauds, and vain,
But all shall be fine and simple
And the beauty of use be plain.
Then art shall be more than jig-work,
And harmony more than show,
And the worth of a thing its measure
In the Age of the Bungalow.

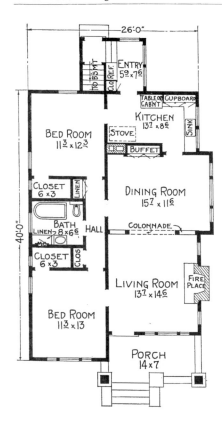

## No. W-95

The desire to keep up appearances often causes people to postpone building a home. Some build fine large homes but put too great a strain on their financial resources. Others build large enough houses, but secure mere size at the sacrifice of the more desirable qualities of conveniences and artistic appearance and desirability.

If a five-room house satisfies present requirements, and one has to conform to the inevitable cost limitation, then this is the kind of a home to build. **BUILD NOW** is good advice. It means to build while the need exists. Most people wait too long to build—defer the thing which the wife and kiddies need most—until the necessity for it has largely passed.

Desirableness—comfort—conveniences—are not matters of size nor always of cost, rather of correct planning. When circumstances change, this home will be salable, usually at a profit.

The plans provide for a half size basement. Walls are siding, the roof shingled and the general construction suitable for reproduction in any climate.

*For costs and plan prices, see pages 56, 57 and 58*

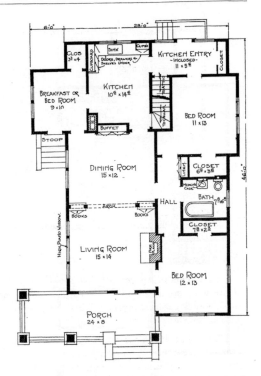

## No. W-96

The extended porch makes this an uncommon Bungalow type. No one ever has too much porch room. Even this porch could be enlarged by running it back and the only change in the appearance would be to make the side gable high like the front one. If a small porch would suffice, the side one can be cut off with a saving of $50. As in most modern houses, the porch floors and steps are cemented; the retaining wall and pedestals are brick.

The plan is remarkable in many ways. The intercommunicating hall is conducive to greatest privacy in the principal rooms. The popular demand for plenty of closets and good sized ones is certainly met in this house. Besides the closets there are all the built-in cabinets that are so necessary in making housekeeping a delight. Access to a large cellar is via the kitchen. The attic is large enough to afford satisfactory storage space and is conveniently reached by stairs from the screen porch.

*For costs and plan prices, see pages 56, 57 and 58*

*Don't take a chance on being shrewd enough to beat the building game. Protection costs so little and pays both contracting parties in the long run.*

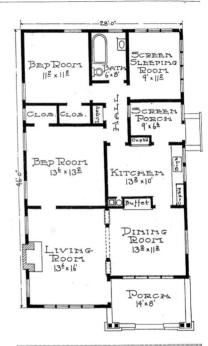

## No. W-97

An exceedingly restful, homelike feeling is characteristic of this Bungalow. One of the very splendid points is the inconspicuous location of the front door. All of the outside walls are shingles with a very light oil stain. The photograph shows what a decorative thing an awning may be.

The plan is for six rooms and large closets; one of the best rooms being the large open-air sleeping room—a feature which is often desired even in very cold climates. The two principal rooms have a massive arch between them with bookcases built into the buttresses. Paneled wainscoting, beamed ceilings and hardwood floors are included in the plans and list of materials. Kitchen conveniences are exceptional. We recommend this particularly as one of our best planned inexpensive homes.

This plan with stairs from back porch to cellar and exterior of W-918 sold at same prices.

*For costs and plan prices, see pages 56, 57 and 58*

*A home is a mirror which reflects the taste of people who build.*

*An artistic home is your best advertisement.*

### No. W-98

Good living porches, even for comparatively small houses, are one of the essentials for existence throughout a very large area of our country.

Here is a Bungalow with front and side porches which add much to the beauty as well as to the comfort of the home. While the terrace parts of the front porch are open to the sky, the pergola beams overhead can be roofed flat by a method that will give protection from the sun and yet preserve the beauty of the pergola design.

The plan is a simple arrangement of five rooms. The immense living room itself conforms to the exterior feeling of comfort. One has every opportunity to develop a wonderfully attractive interior in such a living room and it is well adapted to the needs of those who have a fondness for music and dancing.

The house is of standard frame construction with a basement under the entire rear part back of the living room.

*For costs and plan prices, see pages 56, 57 and 58*

*The Builder who works from a picture and floor plan, unconsciously does the Owner and his own best interests an injustice.*

## No. W-99

In the rivalry for distinctive homes, unique effects can always be had by some very simple applications of details of design to rather unconventional body lines. There is a vital consideration, however, and it is that no builder should attempt reproduction or adaptation without details of design. Too much in the matter of lasting appearance, as well as of cost, is at stake to admit of any guess-work.

In this as well as all our other houses, materials are used that are standard grades and sizes all over the world, except the front windows. A special door or window treatment goes a long way toward making a house "different." However, standard stock sizes may be substituted with good effect.

Should an enclosed entrance be considered necessary, the porch is of such a design that it could easily be enclosed with either glass or screens.

The plan has all the closets and conveniences required and desired. One of the notable features is a Pullman breakfast alcove. The basement is under the rear half of the plan.

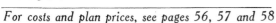

*For costs and plan prices, see pages 56, 57 and 58*

*A good mechanic is worth his price. Stillwell Plans help good mechanics do better work and are also worth the price.*

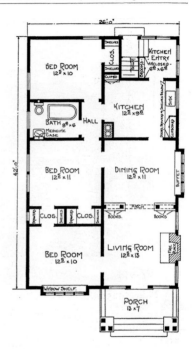

## No. W-910

Here is a neat little Bungalow that is peer to any in its class. Walls and roof are all shingles, verge boards, brackets and porch posts are rough solid timbers. The pure white cement work of the pedestals and white window and door casings are a pleasing contrast with the dark shingle stain. The porch floor and broad steps are concrete.

Interior wood work of the front bed room, living room and dining room is stained slash grain pine and other rooms are dull white enamel. The plastered kitchen walls are white enamel also, making the rooms beautiful and sanitary.

The dining room has a broad, low buffet, the top forming a deep ledge for the high casement windows. The room sizes would in some sections be called small, but care has been taken to preserve good wall spaces, while closets and cupboards are so arranged as to make every foot of space count for more than in the average small house. The house has a full concrete basement back of the line of the dining room.

*Beauty is not a matter of size, space or place, but of plans correct in every particular.*

*For costs and plan prices, see pages 56, 57 and 58*

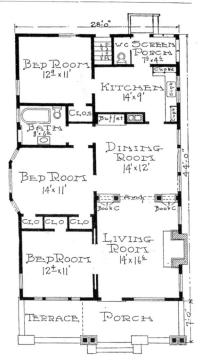

## No. W-911

This Bungalow is also a fine example of the amount of room which may be secured at a reasonable cost. It is built on a forty-foot lot but would show to even better advantage on one somewhat wider. The porch and side gables are shingled. The rear portion has a separate roof which is hipped up behind. Porch and terrace walls are clinker brick with cement caps and the floors cement.

Specifications for the living room and dining room include thin oak flooring, paneled wainscoting, plate rail, beamed ceilings, and sand finished tinted plaster. The fireplace is six feet wide and faced with pressed brick. The columned arch has bookcases with glass doors built into the buttresses. As in all of our plans, the buffet and kitchen cabinet are designed in keeping with the style of the interior finish and suitable to the demands of an ordinary family. The house has three bed rooms and a large closet for each. A grade door at the cellar entrance avoids the necessity of lifting the usual trap doors.

*For costs and plan prices, see pages 56, 57 and 58*

*Stillwell Plans are valuable information and advice in addition to the insurance against trouble.*

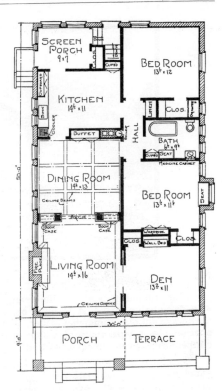

## No. W-912

Brick (or tile) fire-resisting construction is a new development in small houses. The walls of this Bungalow are solid masonry with a thick coating of stucco. The inside studs, joists and rafters are wood, but the roof, different from the ordinary fire risk, is covered with cement tiles. Our plans call for a direct front porch entrance, instead of at the end, as the photograph shows. This makes a great improvement in the front appearance. With a fully developed setting, this will make a strikingly attractive Bungalow. Ordinary frame construction would cost about $250 less.

This is a fully equipped Bungalow, with book cases, buffet, cold air closet, kitchen cabinets, concealed wall bed, drawers in closets, wardrobe, and big screen porch with combination inside and grade entrance to the basement.

*For costs and plan prices, see pages 56, 57 and 58*

*For best results, you need the best plans.*

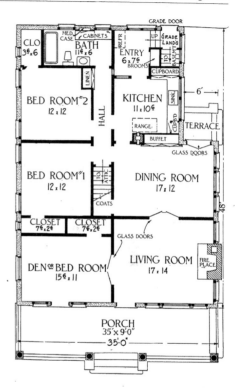

## No. W-913

This white Bungalow is an excellent example of inexpensive design applied to rather a large plan, with walls of hollow tile. The simple, attractive form of the exterior permits the use of tile (or brick) at a cost of about 5 per cent over that of all wood construction.

There is a delightfully cool front porch. A small side entrance with beautiful glass doors adds to the cheerfulness of the dining room and saves frequent travel through the front entrance.

The house is amply supplied with closets and cabinets. In addition, a large attic is made available for storage by having a stairway. This attic is about 8½ feet high in the center and at a width of 10 feet has side walls 6 feet high. Thus two low rooms might be finished off. The first-story ceilings are 8 feet 4 inches high.

One reaches the cellar (or basement) by way of a weather-proof grade landing and this cellar is made the full area of the house back of the living room.

*For costs and plan prices, see pages 56, 57 and 58*

*If you would have no cause for regrets, begin with comprehensive plans from a disinterested source.*

## No. W-914

The time-defying, weather-proof qualities of concrete and tile make them the ideal materials for small as well as for large homes. This little house makes use of these materials and adds a new word to the design of the small house.

The walls are of hollow tile coated with pure white plaster. This combines perfectly with the dark brown trim and red terra cotta tile roof. The pergola-driveway, seemingly an extension of the porch front, makes a comparatively narrow house appear quite wide. Touches of white at the ends of timbers are one of the little details that make the house unusual.

The entrance at the side of the porch leaves a fine lawn unbroken across the front of the house. From the front door one gets a good view of the dining room and the idea of spaciousness is carried out. The basement is excavated under the rear two-thirds of the plan and is divided into five compartments.

*For costs and plan prices, see pages 56, 57 and 58*

*Using Stillwell Plans the Contractor works less, worries less, and earns more; while the Owner gets more for his money.*

## No. W-915

This is another of the stucco wall, tile roof, fire and time resisting houses. The stucco surface in this case is applied to a base of metal lath on wood studding. The walls could be of hollow tile, using the same plans.

The roof is made of genuine terra cotta tile and it is steep enough to make it worth while to arrange for access to the attic by means of a regular stairway.

Every conceivable comfort and convenience is arranged for in the plan. While some of these could be omitted if absolutely necessary in order to build at all, every one of the various features is worth all it costs. We build to better our condition, so it is wise to make the most satisfying job of it.

In this house the foundation is entirely excavated, forming a big basement divided into various compartments. An outside door to the laundry is a desirable feature.

*For costs and plan prices, see pages 56, 57 and 58*

*Stillwell Plans insure the best house at lowest cost*

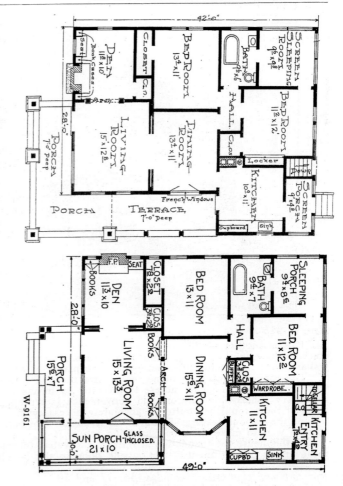

## No. W-916

The exterior of this unique Bungalow is shingled as far down as the window sills and sided below. Porch and terrace floors are cement. Roll roofing covers the house and is of particular advantage in the flattened porch roof. The terrace porch is covered only with pergola beams. There is a cellar which is 12x15 feet.

Plan No. W-9161 has an exterior similar to No. W-916. Working plans will be furnished with or without a basement. The enclosed porch is designed for using both screens and sash, according to season.

*For costs and plan prices, see pages 56, 57 and 58*

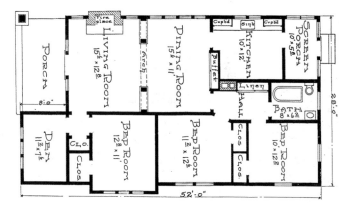

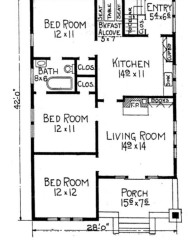

## No. W-917

Here is an attractive Bungalow that can be built cheaply for the number of rooms it contains. The exterior is siding, with a simple treatment of wide boards and battens in the gables. The large plan is set on a low foundation while the floor line of the small plan is 2½ feet above grade.

Plan No. W-917 is a typical arrangement of a six-room Bungalow with the addition of a small den or office.

If cellar plan is desired, this will be furnished with plans without extra charge.

Plan No. W-9171 is an economy plan, affording most of the accommodations of six-room Bungalows. Many housewives prefer to use a breakfast alcove all the time, and so a regular dining room can be dispensed with.

*For costs and plan prices, see pages 56, 57 and 58*

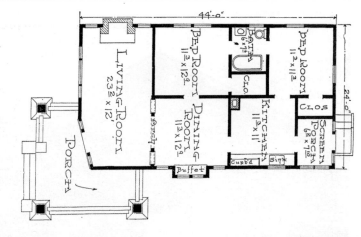

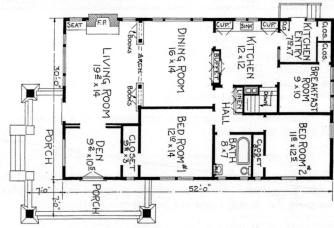

## No. W-918

Of all our Bungalow selections, this house has attracted the most notice. We have fitted this design to many houses of greatly different sizes and arrangement, as these floor plans show.

The exterior is shingled. Although our original plan is only 24 feet wide, the extension of the porch at the side creates an effect of a greater width.

Plan No. W-918 (upper) is made without a cellar, but we furnish a separate foundation plan with stairs from the enclosed back entry, on request.

Plan No. W-9181 is a mighty fine arrangement for a larger house. It provides for a half-size basement with coal, furnace and store rooms. This makes a better looking exterior than the original from which it was modeled.

*For costs and plan prices, see pages 56, 57 and 58*

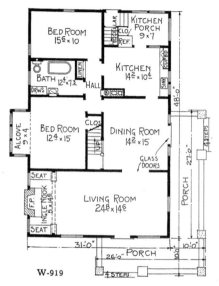

W-919

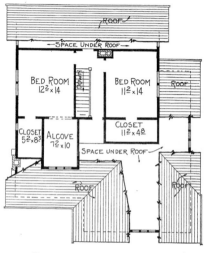

Second-Story Plan No. W-919

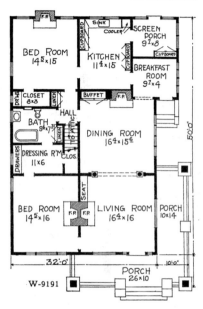

W-9191

## No. W-919

These plans are so much different that they permit a considerable improvement over the exterior design of the original, W-918, after which it is modeled.

Unlike the original, it is gabled high at the sides by running the rafters one way—from front to rear. This produces what is known as a story-and-half house. Half of the second story is a low attic and the center half high enough for rooms. In this case the ceilings are square and 7½ feet high, leaving big storage spaces in front and rear with low windows in them.

The exterior walls are a combination of siding and shingles, the latter being the treatment of front and side gables. The porch columns are stone, square to the beam line and not battered like W-918.

There is a stone basement under all but the living room. It has a furnace room, fuel room and a big laundry with outside steps. Floors are cemented throughout.

*For costs and plan prices, see pages 56, 57 and 58*

## No. W-9191

It is thought necessary in many homes of the South to have fireplaces—or grates, as they are called—in each room. While this is one of the habits in building and has some disadvantages, there are also advantages. Even if more costly than furnace heating, and requiring large rooms, it is an ideal means of ventilation, and the cheering warmth of an open fire is much appreciated.

The exterior design of this house is similar to the one on page 18, but our plans show a better looking house because of the increased size, and the fact that the roof is higher. The 8½-foot high attic has windows in the side gables, but is not finished for rooms. Like the original, the roof is hipped over the rear portion, and then is gabled at the sides over a front span of about 34 feet. Like W-919, it might have high attic rooms if the gabled roof were made to span the entire length from front to rear.

The first story ceilings are 10 feet high. No cellar is provided, but there is a substantial cement block foundation.

### No. W-920

Here is a house with typical Bungalow lines, but showing the influence of the popular Colonial style as applied to small homes.

The Bungalow in its most recent California development is no longer darkly stained. If the body is stained the trim is always smoothed and painted—not rough as at first. This one has a rough siding with a light gray finish, pure white trimmings, and green roof.

Like most all of our other Bungalows, the plans are made with a basement, enclosed stairway, etc., making the house suitable for reproduction in any locality having a variety of climate—hot and cold.

On account of the high cost of building, the house has the minimum of in-built equipment, but everything that is necessary. Instead of one of the long interior halls that are so expensive, this plan has just a small square back hall that provides all necessary accessibility.

*For costs and plan prices, see pages 56, 57 and 58*

*Stillwell plans prevent errors and save builders' time.*

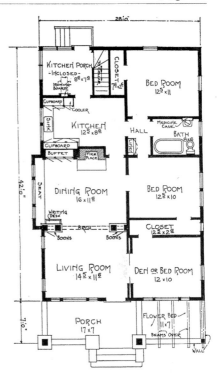

### No. W-921.

In small houses, one has to be dependent almost entirely upon the design of the porch to make the house appeal to the passerby. In this instance artificial stone (cement blocks) are employed and these are of exceptionally good form—rivaling the natural stone. The porch, including the light gray porch pedestals, railing and floor, is all cement work. This is matched by the gray siding and ivory white trimmings on the house. The roof is of wood shingles.

The interior is especially planned with every built-in convenience to make work easy and reduce the cost of furnishing. This is particularly desirable in a house with so little floor and wall space. Occupants of the Bungalow say the kitchen is rather large for simple housekeeping, as almost all of the work is within reach from a piano stool. The general opinion, though, is that it is well to provide space for a breakfast table, as was done here. The kitchen porch is walled and plastered up to a height of three and one-half feet, leaving screened openings that may be enclosed with glass in winter months.

*For costs and plan prices, see pages 56, 57 and 58*

*"Preparedness" in the form of minutely detailed plans is the only guarantee of one hundred per cent. results.*

No. W-922.

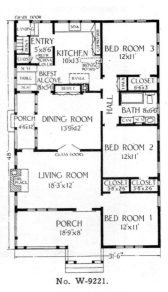

No. W-9221.

## No. W-922

California Bungalows borrow from every architectural style of other countries. So it happens that a house may be a Bungalow in plan only and have an almost pure English cottage exterior like this one. One of the effects of the war already is seen in the English influence, as shown also in the houses on the next page.

The exterior is wide siding over building paper and sheathing. Casement windows are necessary to the front design, but ordinary standard double hung windows may be used on the sides.

A choice of two plans places the design within reach of people of varying circumstances and family requirements. Both give a maximum of space within a comparatively small area. In each plan the cellar extends up to the rear wall of the living room.

*For costs and plan prices, see pages 56, 57 and 58*

*A builder is known by the satisfaction he gives. Satisfaction can be guaranteed only by the use of our complete detail plans.*

*For costs and plan prices, see pages 56, 57 and 58*

## No. W-923

This is an attractive Bungalow showing English influence. It is suitable for an eastern or north frontage. Terraces assume the purpose of ordinary porches. If it should be necessary, the pergola beams of the side terrace may be roofed flat on top. This plan has a half-size basement with inside cellar stairs.

## No. W-9231

A small house may be planned for efficiency and it may be of unique design at small cost. This house has shingled walls and roof. The cement terrace has an edging of brick with a trough arrangement for attractive planting. There is a concrete basement under back of the living room.

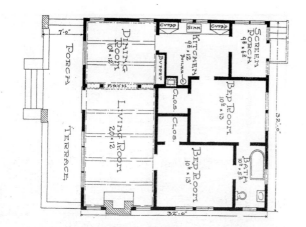

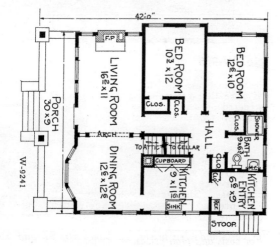

## No. W-924

Here is a specimen of the Bungalow style design for wide frontage effect, although only 32 feet wide. The exterior is siding up to the window tops and the rest shingles. The brick of the porch is laid with raked out joints.

Floor Plan No. W-924 is an economy plan that takes no space for hall or stairways. Regular working plans do not provide for a cellar, but such a plan will be supplied on request.

Floor Plan No. W-9241 is a special plan providing more accessibility with slightly smaller rooms. There is a full-size basement and a 10x29 attic space that is 4½ feet high at the angle of rafters and walls. The exterior has lines similar to the above design. The roof is somewhat higher, which is an improvement.

*For costs and plan prices, see pages 56, 57 and 58*

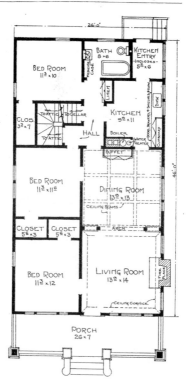

## No. W-925

Every line and detail of this home characterizes it as one of the best specimens of pure Bungalow design. It has a beautiful cement porch with a broad view unobstructed by center post supports. The walls are covered with rough Bungalow siding stained brown. The roof shingles are stained green. The roof is gabled up in front—enough to get head room for a nice attic—while the rear portion has a hip roof.

The plan is a model arrangement for a Bungalow, having the accessibility characteristic of the best California type of Bungalows with the added feature of a stairway to the attic. There are all the built-in necessities—a beautiful buffet, a kitchen cabinet that goes clear to the ceiling, a linen cupboard of the same design, and a medicine case. The water boiler and gas heater are enclosed in an asbestos lined closet. The pressed brick fireplace contributes much to the interior cheerfulness while the columned arch with its broad opening gives spaciousness to the two principal rooms.

*For costs and plan prices, see pages 56, 57 and 58*

*As a class, contractors are honest. But good intentions never compensate for disappointing results. The best results are certain with Stillwell Plans.*

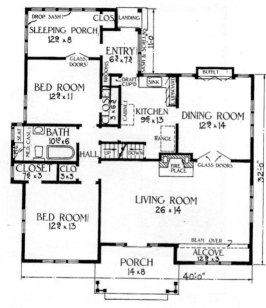

## No. W-926

If one has a lot of 60 feet or more, a wide-front Bungalow should be selected. A broad front offers better opportunity for individual design. This is a home that is distinctive because of its simple lines, clean-cut detail and careful window treatment. The clipping off of the gable peaks shortens the long ridge line to just the correct proportions.

The arrangement of rooms is far different from most 5-room houses. In accordance with the present-day tendency, the living room is extra large. Other rooms are of good size, and all principal rooms get light and ventilation from two sides.

A bungalow attic is necessarily low, but if made accessible by only a steep stairway, like this one, it is very useful. In the plan a flight of cellar stairs goes down from the kitchen to a basement that is about one-half the area of the plan. In the South and other sections where a cellar is not desired, the stair space can be used as a store closet.

*For costs and plan prices, see pages 56, 57 and 58*

*Truly successful building under-takings are invariably the result of careful planning. You will save money, too, in the end by spending a little in advance.*

## No. W-927

As has often been pointed out, for a one-story dwelling, the bungalow style offers the widest range for selection.

This one is a splendid example of the "something different" idea—and people are naturally desirous of having their own home express individuality. The English type of hooded entrance with half-timber gable makes the design unique.

The exterior is siding, and all the porch and foundation work is concrete. The front windows are casements, but the common sliding type would also do well. Blinds are used in front and are intended for effect rather than for real use.

This plan is notable in that three of the five main rooms have a view of the street. Also, the rooms are rather larger than those of a small house in the North. The corner porch is liked by many people because it is so easily screened from public view. There is a small basement for a furnace, and the fireplace chimney is used for all flues.

*For costs and plan prices, see pages 56, 57 and 58*

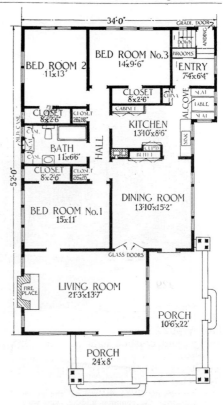

## No. W-928

The flat roofed Bungalows have one feature of design that creates for them a distinct preference over other types. This advantage lies in the fact that wide porches, such as this house has, can be effectively and economically roofed even though the spans are wide.

To those not familiar with them, they may not seem strong enough nor steep enough, but they are. The roof is built up on the principle of the tar-and-gravel roof of flatter roofed commercial buildings, only some better looking material than gravel or slag is used for surfacing. This is often crushed brick, as in this instance, or crushed granite screenings to make a glistening effect.

The lowness of the attic naturally would make it hotter than a high one, were it not for the fact that a surfaced roof reflects much of the sun heat, whereas shingles draw heat. In such houses special ventilators are always built in the peaks of the gable ends.

Aside from the roof feature (and this itself is no objection), the house is built the same as any other cold climate Bungalow.

*For costs and plan prices, see pages 56, 57 and 58*

*Contractors like Stillwell Plans because they eliminate controversy and please the Owner.*

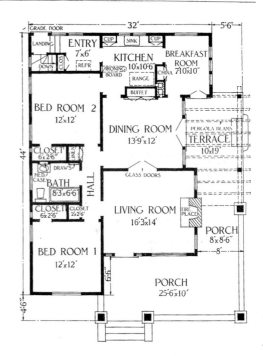

## No. W-929

Sometimes the flat roofed houses are called "Swiss Chalet" Bungalows, although this is not a correct term for them. This specimen is one of the finest of its kind.

It has porch walls of buff-brown brick, light buff plaster walls, pure white trimmings, and crushed light granite screenings for the roof surfacing.

The inviting comfort of the spacious porches makes the Bungalow exceptionally attractive. These porches are all floored with concrete. The purpose of the side terrace is to let light into the dining room, but a flat roof could be laid on top of the beams without altering the pergola effect.

In the plan nothing that is needed for the comfort or convenience of the housewife has been overlooked. Rooms are all of good average proportions, but these may be expanded, as necessary in hot climates, by increasing the over-all length and width. The house has a basement under the rear half of the plan, making it practicable for reproduction in cold or semi-cold climates.

*For costs and plan prices, see pages 56, 57 and 58*

*Builders' amateur plans purporting to reproduce our houses cannot fail to be inferior. Safety first is a good rule. Get plans from original sources and save money.*

## No. W-930

    This house is popularly known as the one-story Swiss Chalet type. About the only difference between it and ordinary Bungalows is style of the roof. The roof has a low pitch that is characteristic of the homes of the Swiss people. The wide overhang or cornice is supported by heavy timbers that form a part of the frame of the building. The covering is a red composition roofing that is fully guaranteed and that has proven satisfactory on roofs of lowest pitch under all conditions, when properly laid. The walls of the house are wide and narrow siding. The white cement work of the porch is consistently carried out, being continued across the entire front of the bed room in a most pleasing way that gives an effect of massiveness and strength to the building. The broad fireplace carries out the same idea.

    The interior is a simple arrangement of five rooms with all modern built-in cabinet work. Bed rooms, kitchen and bath are finished in ivory white enamel. Living room and dining room in light Flemish stained pine. Plans furnished with a small cellar in rear with outside steps.

*For costs and plan prices, see pages 56, 57 and 58*

*The real test of Stillwell homes comes from that satisfaction of Owners which lasts long after the mere cost of plans is forgotten.*

# PRACTICAL SERVICEABILITY *of* STILLWELL-PLANNED CALIFORNIA HOMES
## EASILY ADAPTED TO MEET ALL CLIMATIC CONDITIONS

The beautiful homes of California are a natural product of the Pacific Coast. A wide range of climatic and site conditions furnish a variety of settings for ideal homes.

A kindly climate and a beautiful land promotes originality in architecture. The classic architectural forms of ancient Greece, Rome and the other Mediterranean countries, were adopted throughout the world and adapted to the varying conditions of climate. So have California style homes—the bungalow in particular—been found practical under the severest tests and accepted as a distinctly American architectural style.

Yet few people outside of California and the tourist class understand what bungalows really are. A prolific source of misinformation about bungalows is the publication of some good bungalow pictures secured through Los Angeles photographers, but accompanied by plans that do not fit and do not reproduce the original exteriors if built from. Most of the so-called bungalows, Eastern built, that are illustrated in various publications are so unattractive as to give many prospective builders of artistic tastes an entirely false conception of the beauties and advantages of California homes and bungalows in particular.

The average North American home has to provide for a combination of climates—extremely hot in summer and bitter cold in winter. The homes of the Pacific Coast that are shown in Stillwell publications are, for the most part, perfectly adaptable to the requirements of cold climates.

All of these houses have solid foundations—usually concrete. Most of them have cellars or basements which provide for heating equipment. The same kinds and sizes of timber and other materials are specified for construction as are universally used.

Local conditions may require such changes as the elimination or addition of insulating papers, sheathing, or change of size or depth of foundations. These more or less concealed details of construction in most cases can be arranged by the builder to suit the owner. Specifications therefor are left open for individual selection in our specification blanks. Other changes as to arrangement can often be specified in the building contract or in a supplementary sheet attached to specifications.

In all our plans, provision is made for screening all windows with full length screens. Where screened sleeping porches are not provided, bedrooms may be equipped with hinged casement sashes, or with disappearing (drop) sashes or more of the double sliding type of windows added. In most cases, sleeping porches may be built out from bedrooms without affecting the original plan.

Very few of our plans provide for vestibules as they spoil the arrangement of a small plan and do not look well. But winter vestibules can be made to set up in sections. Front porches may be glassed or screened in according to season and location.

Every one of our plans show a screened porch or enclosed entry. These are rooms which are considered indispensible in warm climates and are even more necessary in cold climates. These porches, or rather rear entrance halls or vestibules, are studded up and have walls the same as any room. Openings are high, which feature shuts out the hot sun, dust, rain or snow, allows the full use of the wall and floor spaces and effectually conceals the interior. The screen openings are so made that they can be equipped with winter sash and storm doors. Thus the glass enclosed screen porch serves as a rear vestibule and often provides a very comfortable basement stairway location which does not interfere with the convenient arrangement of other rooms. Dirt is not tracked through the kitchen and proper ventilation is secured.

Sunshine is both a germicide and nerve tonic, so the large window area which is so characteristic of California homes is equally desirable in other climates. If this increases the cost of heating, it is a **healthful** measure and less expensive than doctors' bills. It also promotes dryness within. The wide overhang or roof extension of these homes shields outside walls from the intense heat of the summer sun at mid-day. When the sun is low in winter, the roof is high enough to admit his cheering warmth.

The height of most first story ceilings in these houses are between 9 and 10 feet—the average American room height. Second story ceilings are 8 feet high. For the South and Southwest, ceilings may be raised to conform to custom if desired.

By increasing the width and length of floor plans, this will, with higher ceilings, give the spaciousness of open rooms and halls which add to comfort during the long heated period. But the cost of building is greatly increased thereby as is also the expense of furnishing. It is often better to save by building on a medium size plan, but giving special attention to the ventilation of overhead attic and under-floor spaces.

By exercising a little ingenuity, any builder can use our ready-made working plans for building homes in any part of the country. To enable builders to use these low cost stock plans, we are always glad to offer suggestions as to changes. Where extensive departures from the original plans make it advisable to have special plans prepared, we will do this for a reasonable fee.

# A MAN BUILT EIGHT
## STILLWELL BUNGALOWS

Used ready-made plans.    This letter is an unsolicited testimonial.)

Gentlemen:                      Edwardsville, Ill.
I mailed you a check a few days ago for
$10,00, covering the plans sent me October 23rd.
I received the two books and thank you very
much for them.  I have built eight California
Bungalows in one block this last summer, and
they are the first genuine Bungalows that have
been built in this locality.  Some fifteen hundred
people have visited them during the last three
weeks and they have created considerable ex-
citement.  For your information I am sending
you one of the circulars I got up announcing
the completion of them.
I have a great many Bungalow books, but I
have found nothing that is as complete in every
detail as the plans shown in your booklets.  You
certainly have the proposition down to perfec-
tion.                              S. F. LLOYD.

**STILLWELL BUNGALOWS IN ILLINOIS**

# THE MODERN BUNGALOW HOME

Nothing in recent years that so completely affects home life
has grown so rapidly in favor as nas the modern Bungalow. First
from the West and South, and now from the East and North,
comes the unqualified approval and adoption of this style of home.

**We are all inclined to question the merits of most things upon
which we are not informed.** This has been true to some extent with
the Bungalow, but these objections are quickly eliminated when an
investigation is made.

In this section of the middle West, where we have a combination of climates, **many builders modify the plans and constructions
of the Bungalow until it loses its identity.** This, while it may not
destroy its many advantages, does destroy its beauty and denies the
extra satisfaction and comfort which a combination of beauty and
convenience affords.

One hears nearly every type of country and suburban home
called a Bungalow, provided only that the house is somewhat in-
formal or picturesque in its lines.  Some one has remarked that in
the new dictionaries a Bungalow should be defined as "a house
that looks as if it had been built for less money than it actually
cost."

Simple as a Bungalow appears outwardly, an economical
arrangement of living room, dining room, service and bed rooms,
with means of ready communication is not easily accomplished.  It
is not uncommon to find an otherwise attractive Bungalow with **25
percent of the floor space wasted.**

With all due respect to the complete knowledge that every
new builder of a home has, as to just what is right and proper, it
must be admitted that the architectural profession deserves a
large place in the arrangement, if the **best results** are to be obtained.
It is well then to go fully into every detail and feature of the plans
before changing or discarding them.

The Bungalow must be long, low, plain and massive.  To de-
viate from any of these on account of cost, or for any cause,

destroys the true Bungalow effect, while to get these effects and carry them out in **every detail requires the most careful planning.**

Some have thought that the Bungalow, with its wide departure from our cottage and two-story type of house was only a fad and would pass as other fads do. Such opinions are without foundation, for the Bungalow is here to stay. Beautiful in lines, substantial in construction, and practical for health and convenience, it has taken its place as one of the best styles of American homes.

# The Building in Edwardsville of the First Genuine Thoroughly Modern Bungalows

After a very careful study of all the styles of architecture of moderate priced homes, I became convinced there was nothing that could compare with the Bungalow, and with the purchase of the spacious grounds that are now Logan Place, I was afforded the most desirable location for the building of such homes. To-day, five months after starting, eight modern Bungalows, of six and eight rooms each, grace this beautiful park.

The plans for these Bungalows were drawn by Los Angeles, California, architects and but for some minor changes, the finished buildings are just what you would see if you were upon the streets of that most beautiful city, where you can ride a hundred miles and pass nothing but Bungalows.

The deep satisfaction and delight it has given me to plan and build these homes, with their beautiful surroundings, fills me with the desire to have every one interested in the ideal, visit them, and I invite all to come and see, that they may learn the merit and many advantages of the Bungalow.

**Far too often the builder of a new home is disappointed with it;** some important feature or the quality of some material has been overlooked, while a desire to get something cheap leads to a cheapening all along the line, with the result that the home, when finished, falls short of expectations. This is a severe disappointment, for **if there is anything in all the world that concerns one vitally, it is one's own home.**

Although we may build ever so many houses we will always find room for improvement, but experience becomes more valuable here, perhaps, than anywhere else in all the vocations of life, more valuable because it concerns the most vital work.

If you are once interested in a home you will see how completely the objectionable features in building have been eliminated in the construction of the Logan Place Bungalows, and also how many features are added that make up the perfect house.

The arrangement in these houses is considered by the many who have inspected them to be as near perfect as is possible in houses of this size and cost. Every feature that could possibly be included will be found, every inch of space that could be utilized has been wisely used.

**S. F. LLOYD.**

# Who Is Best Qualified to Draw Your Plans?

It is an attribute of human nature to desire the good opinion of others, hence every home owner wishes his house to be attractive.

The exterior is seen by all passers by and their idea of the interior is apt to be formed from the appearance of the exterior. People who consider appearances and appreciate the advantages of an interior planned for convenience and comfort are careful to retain the best talent to make plans for their homes.

The most important consideration from the viewpoint of the owner contemplating the erection of a small home is the expense. For this reason he often feels that he cannot afford the services of a regular architect.

This seems to make it necessary for the contractor to draw the plans. All contractors of wide experience agree that they can not afford to devote much of their time to this phase of their work. Very few are qualified for it. None would attempt it were it not so often necessary just to land the jobs.

The architect of restricted local practice can not afford to neglect larger work to draw small house plans at any price. If you have less than $5,000 to put into a home, it is not likely that you can secure the best service from any local architect.

Ordinary architects are trained for big work and are not much interested in the planning of small buildings. The planning of homes is a specialty and styles are changing from year to year. This requires constant study and special training which the average architect lacks.

Who, then, is qualified to draw your plans at a price you can afford to pay?

Unless local conditions are such as to require personal supervision of the job by a local man, we can render a better service than a local architect. At your disposal is our many years of experience covering this whole country. We specialize on homes. We have a general working knowledge of all conditions of climate. We save owners real money because we are experts and plan homes to be built economically. Unlike specialists of most professions, our experience and volume of business makes it possible for a prospective builder to engage our services for much less than those of a general practitioner.

Stillwell plans assure you the protection you need before you start to build.

# SEND FOR PLANS ON APPROVAL

## SATISFACTORY BUILDING COST GUARANTEED

No contractor can tell you what any house in this book should cost until he sees the detailed working plans and specifications.

A builder is not a mind reader. He must have something definite to figure on with any accuracy. Contracting is enough of a gamble under existing conditions. It is worse than a gamble financially and usually disastrous to the owner when a builder attempts to build without plans a house with which he is not familiar.

For your own protection now—for your own satisfaction in the long, long years to come—don't take any chances. Have definite plans, incorporating your own ideas; that is the only way to get a dollar's worth for a dollar. The great war has taught us that careful preparation is essential for success in any undertaking.

This is no time to guess or to trust to luck. The farmer tests his seed corn; the manufacturer buys only tested and tried materials. Bankers take no man's word for anything—every business proposition goes down in black-and-white. Building a home is strictly a business proposition. Treat it as such with cold business-like judgment.

## GET PLANS AND TEST THEM

Use your own common sense; don't accept any contractor's statement that he doesn't need plans. They all need plans and it is a bad sign if any contractor opposes architects' plans before he has seen them. You need plans to settle and clarify your own ideas if for nothing more.

Plans are the logical starting point for any

---

**FERDINAND FISH**
Mayhew Avenue
Larchmont Park
**Larchmont, New York**

January 26, 1916.

I repeat what I have already said to you a year ago, that I regard your plans as the most practical of any I have used. They are workable in every respect, but the chief charm to me lies in your method of detailing. Usually much is left to the genius and taste or conception of the foreman, or the mill, and as a rule, they have to do a lot of drafting and submitting of sketches in order to get an interpretation of the purpose of the architect. I am an architect and builder of over thirty-five years' experience and I am frank to say that, while I am occasionally compelled to do designing, I find your plans all that I could wish and I would never touch a pencil if I could help it for low-cost houses while I can get what you offer at such prices. My time is worth more on other work. With one exception, I consider that you have no real rival in the interesting field you cover so efficiently. You are welcome to make any use of this letter you wish, as I believe worthy effort should be recognized.

FERDINAND FISH.
Larchmont Park,
Larchmont, New York.

---

building operation. If on account of cost, you are not fully decided, get plans anyway—at least ready-made plans. That will give you something definite to figure on as a basis.

You can send for any of the plans in this book under any one of our five offers as stated on page 57. Every one of these is a money-back offer so you get the plans on approval. Note that offer number four is especially liberal. Send a certified personal check which we will hold long enough to give you 10 days' examination of plans plus the necessary time for transmission of mails. If you want to return the plans within that time, we will return your check. That will give you 10 days—a week and a half—to decide what you want to do. In that time several builders can give you the actual cost of building in your community, built as you want it built. Apply the acid test to our arguments in favor of plans and we will risk your judgment.

## SEE SIDE VIEWS AND INTERIORS

We can not send other photos of exteriors or interiors. The plans will give you an adequate conception of the side and rear views. The interior details of each house are very interesting. You should study them. . . . Write for plans—on suspicion, as Elbert Hubbard would say—in accordance with our offers.

## No. W-935

This is one of our most delightfully simple Bungalows in an attractive setting. A broad porch is enclosed with a cobblestone wall. The exterior finish is plain. Eyebrow louvre ventilators look well and serve to ventilate the attic space.

This is one of the best five-room plans ever devised. Every room is of fairly comfortable dimensions and privacy of bedrooms is observed. The built-in cabinet work which so much simplifies housekeeping, includes book cases, buffet, medicine case, linen cabinet, kitchen cupboards and cold air closet.

This house shows the growing tendency to more and larger windows, admitting more light and air for the better health of the family. A concrete cellar 13 feet square is reached by means of an outside concrete stairway.

*For costs and plan prices, see pages 56, 57 and 58*

## No. W-936

There is a big demand for really cheap houses. But most "cheap" houses show up their quality, if not when new, very soon after. It costs an insignificant amount more to build one that will stand up and look well a long time than one in which depreciation sets in early. Usually it is a matter of careful planning and simple exterior lines of which this bungalow is a good example.

The house has a plain siding exterior including the porch and steps enclosures. The porch floor and steps are wood, a very slight economy over concrete. The roof is a simple span from front to back, giving height for two nice attic rooms. A saving of about $25.00 could be made in eliminating the roof dormer. This adds so much to the appearance and is a necessary means of ventilating the attic and the bed rooms so it is a justifiable investment.

The sun porch in front is rather an unusual feature and is suitable for a beach exposure as well as an inland location. The plan is the simplest possible arrangement and nothing can be arranged any cheaper to build.

*For costs and plan prices, see pages 56, 57 and 58*

*It will cost less to buy Stillwell Plans than to get along without them. Mistakes cost money.*

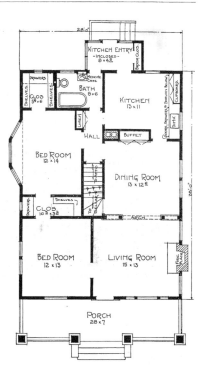

## No. W-937

Many men find that they can turn vacations and out-of-office time to profitable account by building small Bungalows. Attractive homes like this can always be sold at a profit.

This house has walls of siding, a brick-and-cement porch and shingle roof. The rafters span the full length of the plan and form a great big attic. Our plans call for a somewhat greater pitch than the cut shows. This attic is unfinished, but has windows and partitions set for two bed rooms and a store room (in front gable). There is a two-thirds basement divided into rooms.

We also have plans of this house of the same arrangement made to meet the severest cold climate requirements. It has a full-size basement with grade landing entrance to the enclosed back porch and basement. It has two finished second-story bed rooms and the front porch is entirely enclosed with hinged windows.

*For costs and plan prices, see pages 56, 57 and 58*

*You can get along without Stillwell plans, but you can get visibly better results with them.*

## No. W-938

This house is one of the earliest types of Bungalow architecture and borders closely on the older cottage style. But beauty in homes never grows old, no matter how other styles may change. The house stands on a low brick foundation, but the floor is the usual height above grade. The porch steps are concrete and the floor is wood. Walls are rough Bungalow siding painted gray. The wide overhang of the roof shows fancy curved rafter ends supporting molded galvanized iron hanging gutters.

The low out-set window ledge and quintuple casements with transoms make a most satisfying living room. One of the superior points in the plan is the situation of the dining room in front, rather a difficult thing to arrange with economy of space in most Bungalows. Presenting a broad front, this is one of the most impressive five-room houses.

*For costs and plan prices, see pages 56, 57 and 58*

*Stillwell Plans are a form of building insurance with the combination feature that you get more than your money back in the extra selling value of your house.*

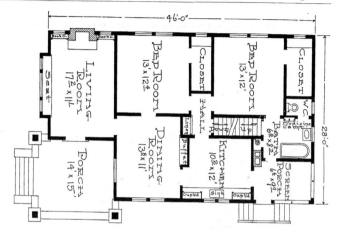

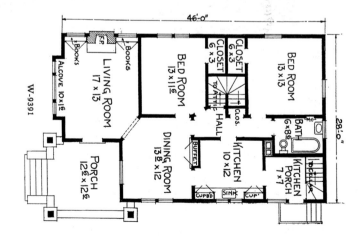

## No. W-939

    The exterior walls are siding, and the roof shingles. The porch shows a fine job of cobblestone work with cemented floor and steps. The plans call for slightly more roof pitch than the cut indicates, which provides for a big storage attic that is about 8 feet high in the center. Another dormer like the one in front could be built out on one side for a sleeping porch.

    Plan No. W-939 (upper) is our original plan for this exterior. It has a cellar 13½ x 16½ under the kitchen, bath and screen porch.

## No. W-9391

    An alternate plan with a full-size, cold climate basement.

*For costs and plan prices, see pages 56, 57 and 58*

## No. W-940

A substantial-looking house, and artistic in every detail. Hundreds of this style of bungalow are built in Los Angeles with endless variations in details and plans, the general lines of the houses remaining the same. The stone veneer extends across the front only, the rest of the house being wide, rough vertical boards and battens to the window sills and shingles above. All exterior wood work is stained.

The bungalow is conveniently planned. The living room might be made smaller, and a den or music room nine feet wide taken off the end. The living room and dining room walls are paneled with upright wide boards and battens to a height of four and one-half feet. This house will be a continual delight to a lover of a good home.

*For costs and plan prices, see pages 56, 57 and 58*

*An ounce of prevention
is worth a pound of cure*

**No. W-941**

The exterior of this beautiful home is a pleasing combination of the least expensive of materials. Porch and fireplace masonry are cobblestones of various colors and uneven sizes, laid up in dark mortar. Walls are shingles which are oiled with a light brown stain. All trimmings are smooth and painted dark brown. Dormers on each side of the roof make the Bungalow as attractive in perspective as directly in front.

This home has the uncommon feature of an entrance hall set off by an attractive arched opening into the living room. One wouldn't ask for greater accessibility between rooms. Being inter-communicating, heating with a furnace is a simple matter, and in summer it is equally easy to keep the rooms cool by cross ventilation through so many opening windows. The combined enclosed porch and basement entrance is a worthy convenience and offers complete protection from the weather.

*For costs and plan prices, see pages 56, 57 and 58*

*Insufficient plans are cheap, but you pay big when you use them*

## No. W-942

This California Bungalow reproduced in a colder climate meets every requirement perfectly; there is no question about that, says the Builder. The plan is a slight deviation from the typical Bungalow arrangement, but has similar conveniences.

The foundation wall is brick while the exterior is cement plaster on metal lath. The roof is good cedar shingles with hanging gutters.

A seven-foot basement under the rear, back of the dining room, is reached by a grade level landing. The porch steps, being inside the glassed-in screen porch, are safe from slippery ice and sleet. This combination grade-door is a comfortable inside entrance arranged in such a way that the necessity of a second or outside cellar stairway is eliminated. The plan has many obviously valuable features and the exterior is of such a beautifully simple design that it is worthy of serious consideration to anyone about to build.

*For costs and plan prices, see pages 56, 57 and 58*

*Stucco can be substituted for siding in any bungalow*

## No. W-943

A bit out of the ordinary—if the design is handled with judgment, avoiding oddity—is always refreshingly interesting. This design borrows just a little from the Spanish—in the secluded little porch and corner entrance garden.

Consider what space and convenience and accessibility is compressed into so small an area. There is nothing cramped about it, all rooms and closets being of fair size. While the actual area of the kitchen is small, the fact that everything is compassed in a small space makes it all the more desirable. That saves miles of steps for the woman who does her own work, as there are plenty of places to put things, and the cupboards are almost within arm's reach of the stove and sink.

The exterior is buff stucco applied to metal lath on a wood frame. The roof is shingled. The basement is under all the house except the front bed room.

*For costs and plan prices, see pages 56, 57 and 58*

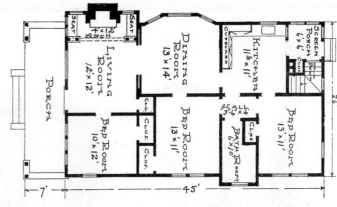

## No. W-944

This is one of the more extreme California Bungalow types. The exterior is all shingles, slightly stained. Working plans call for increased roof pitch to conform to general climatic requirements.

Plan No. W-944 is our original arrangement. The special feature is an inglenook at the end of the living room, with a roof jutting out under the main roof. This nook may be eliminated, making the living room about 14½x12. There is a 11½x17 cellar.

Plan No. W-9441 is for solid brick wall construction, except for the gables, which are shingled. There is a basement extending up as far as the living room.

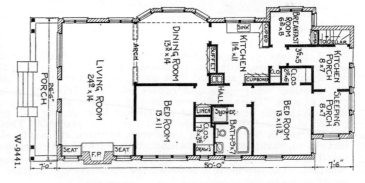

*For costs and plan prices, see pages 56, 57 and 58*

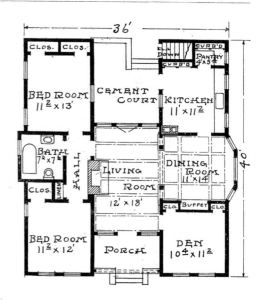

## No. W-945

California furnishes many beautiful examples of large houses in the so-called mission style, but very few really artistic small homes. This is the best example we have of the mission style exterior for a six-room house. The walls are framed up, sheathed, papered and plastered. The front windows are casements opening in. The roof is shingled and has tile hips and ridges. This is cheaper and on a small house looks about as well as an all tile roof.

The plan is that of a letter "H." The den is so situated that it can be used as a bed room. As the two main parts of the house are separated, a third bed room could be built on at the rear of either side. Some builders do not require a cellar; in which case the cupboard and stair space can be turned into a screened entrance.

*For costs and plan prices, see pages 56, 57 and 58*

*The average man doesn't know what a set of plans is, so he is quite apt to regard it as money thrown away. If you are willing to be shown, we will gladly send a set of Stillwell Plans to any bank or express office, with the privilege of fullest examination.*

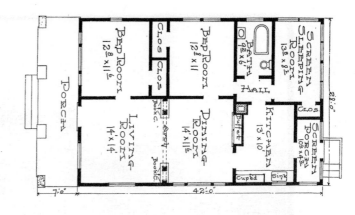

## No. W-946

This Bungalow is simplicity itself, but really "classy" and not at all suggestive of the inexpensiveness of its construction. The walls are stained wide siding, but the porch gable has a finish of shingles. The porch floor is cemented and the heavy columns supporting the roof are cement blocks.

There are practically six rooms, as the sleeping porch is large and may be enclosed with hinged or disappearing sash which drop into the walls. There is no cellar under the original house, but we have an extra foundation plan with outside steps to a cellar under the back porch and kitchen.

Floor Plan No. W-9461 is a special plan with a similar exterior, except the roof is much steeper. This is built of solid brick. There is a half-size basement entered by stairs from a grade landing off from the enclosed porch.

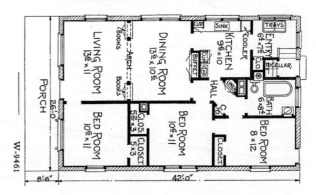

*For costs and plan prices, see pages 56, 57 and 58*

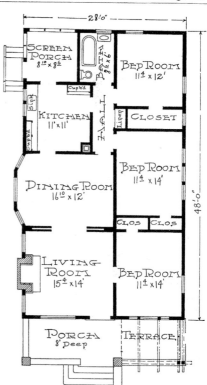

## No. W-947

Here is a typical Bungalow of six large rooms built cheaply and well. It has a plain gable roof with an extension of it over the porch. There are lattice ventilators in each gable. The siding is stained a dark brown and trimmings are painted. The house is set well above ground on a high terraced lot. Porch and terrace walls are brick with cement floors and steps.

The front door is one of the stock bungalow styles, wide and heavy. The wide living room window is plate glass. The style of the front bed room window is a little different, being cut up with a center light and small casements on either side. This room can be very easily fitted up as a den, if desired. Special notice should be taken of the grouping of the four rooms and bath about the pass hall. This Bungalow has no cellar, but an excavation of good size with an outside entrance can be made at very low cost. The kitchen fixtures include a cooler having screened shelves, a cold air duct under the house and a ventilating flue up through the roof.

*Wherever you live, we can draw your plans.*

*For costs and plan prices, see pages 56, 57 and 58*

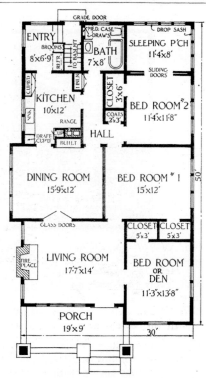

## No. W-948

The open cornice—gabled end—stained wood Bungalow is now and for years has been the least expensive type to build. While styles may change more or less, this kind will be found pre-eminently suitable for many conditions and circumstances. The workmanship is simple and the long straight lines require the least labor. This is a cost factor that should not be overlooked when making a home investment.

It will be noticed that cement blocks of pleasing forms are used for the porch and chimneys. It is important that such blocks closely resemble natural stone; otherwise it is much better to use brick or stucco than much of the unattractive cement block work one sees in most communities. Instead of siding between the low foundation and the floor line as seen in the picture, our new plans provide for a good solid concrete wall up to the joists. There is a concrete basement under the rear half of the plan.

*For costs and plan prices, see pages 56, 57 and 58*

*Good intentions never assure results. Let your builder build only from Stillwell proven plans.*

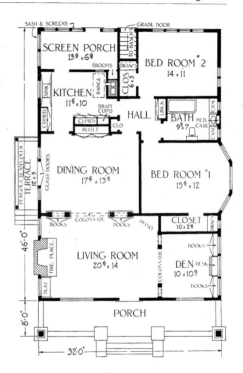

## No. W-949

In the design of this Bungalow we have considered the matter of first cost with unusual care. That is why the simple gabled roof is run from front to back over the entire length. This does not make a plain looking house, because small side gables over the fireplace and bay window effectually break up the long lines.

The house stands on a concrete foundation well above grade. The porch work is all of cement, the cement floor being considered better and as cheap as wood. The outer walls are siding except shingles are used in the front gable for variation.

The interior is a typical Bungalow plan with an unusual amount of built-in equipment. Of course so much mill work is costly, but one must furnish a house anyway, and bookcases, desks, etc., offset a considerable part of this expense.

This house was planned with a 10x17 cellar for a furnace room under the hall and bath. The stairs go down from the outside only, but the enclosed kitchen porch is large enough for inside steps with a grade landing.

*For costs and plan prices, see pages 56, 57 and 58*

*Contractors are men of honor and unusual qualifications, but often treated with distrust. Stillwell plans are made to forestall any misunderstandings.*

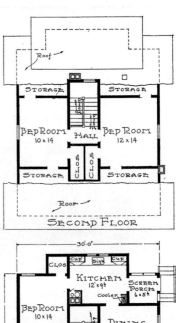

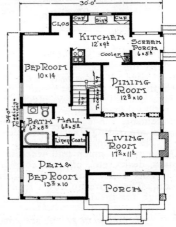

No. W-950

The expansive roof of this house covers a surprisingly large amount of floor space. The partly recessed porch and large well placed windows with the beautiful surroundings make this a most attractive home.

The living room and dining room are separated with a wide columned arch. The front room which is shut off from the living room by a sliding door can be made a sun parlor, den or an emergency bed room. One of the best things in these plans is the hall which connects the principal rooms below and also forms a convenient means of reaching the rooms above. The stairs being cut off from the living room will not carry off heat as they do in most open stairways. Some of the nice points about this Bungalow are the large closets, kitchen cupboards, ventilated cooling closet, medicine cabinet built in the bath room, and the basement.

*For costs and plan prices, see pages 56, 57 and 58*

## No. W-951

An artistic, just finished Bungalow—embodying some of the latest ideas in design —that will be even more pleasing in a fully developed setting. The porch work is gray sand-lime brick with white mortar joints. The walls are alternating wide and narrow widths of surfaced siding painted gray with pure white trimmings. Roof gutters are of the inconspicuous "hanging" type and supported by projecting rafter ends. The roof is brown stained shingles.

The plan is rather an unusual arrangement, affording the utmost comfort in a five-room Bungalow. With a view to conserving wall and floor space the fireplace is located in a corner of the living room and the brick mantel projects but four inches. An arch of the columned and buttress type separates the living room and dining room. The commodious kitchen cupboard is a noteworthy feature of this home. This is built from floor to ceiling, the upper side cupboards being suspended above a wide work counter and drain boards. The cellar is located under the second bed room.

*For costs and plan prices, see pages 56, 57 and 58*

*Contractors do not like to draw plans. With those who do, it's only a matter of expediency— getting your name signed to the dotted line. For a house of no regrets, get a third party's plans —Stillwell Plans*

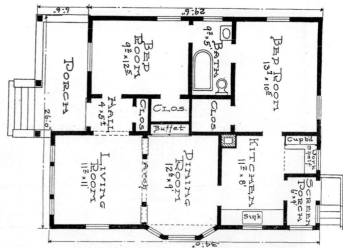

No. W-952

This picture shows one of the most pleasing types of small Bungalow homes. It looks big for its moderate cost. The walls are six-inch stained siding trimmed with cream color paint.

Plan No. W-952 is an arrangement that has been tried out and it has pleased many people. It is more on the cottage order, having an entrance hall and pantry. There is no cellar in complete plans, but a supplementary foundation provides one where needed.

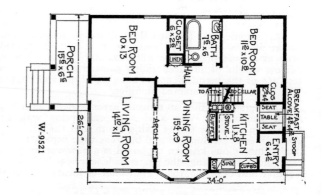

Plan No. W-9521 (lower) is a new alternate plan. It was especially prepared to accommodate the popular need for stairways and breakfast alcoves. There is a full-size basement.

*For costs and plan prices, see pages 56, 57 and 58*

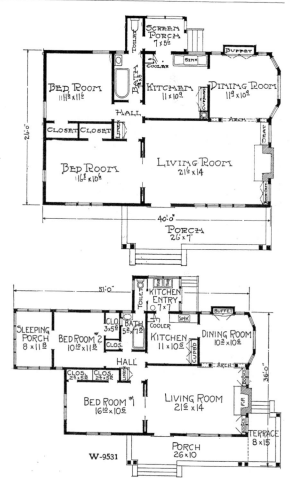

## No. W-953

Wide front Bungalows are very popular where people have enough lot frontage. They make a more impressive appearance with the length showing in the front elevation. This house has walls of siding, a shingle roof and wood porch floors.

Floor Plan No. W-953 is our original arrangement. There is no cellar, but cellar stairs, if desired, might be taken off the back porch.

Floor Plan No. W-9531 is a revised plan of the same house, affording more closet room and a sleeping porch. It has no cellar or basement. This is a particularly good plan for a country home in a mild climate.

*For costs and plan prices, see pages 56, 57 and 58*

### No. W-954

It is fine to have a wide lot so that three of one's living rooms may be planned in front to take advantage of the outlook. It is a double advantage to have such a splendid living porch. The cellar in this house is about half size.

### No. W-9541

Wide fronts make comparatively small bungalows appear quite large. An impression of interior spaciousness comes from having the front rooms connected by wide sliding doors which are generally open. There is a cellar under bath and kitchen.

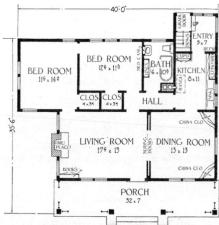

*For costs and plan prices, see pages 56, 57 and 58*

*For costs and plan prices, see pages 56, 57 and 58*

## No. W-955

Wide houses like this are preferable for wide lots and in the country. This is an open-air house as all rooms but the kitchen have double wall exposure with plenty of windows. While expressly designed for warm weather comfort, there is also a good basement for furnace heating.

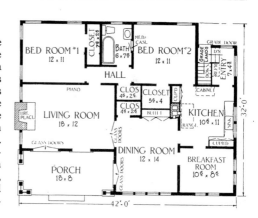

## No. W-9551

This is a homey looking white Bungalow with round columns, more of which types are shown in our book of "The New Colonials," described in the back cover. One seldom sees a 5-room house of this width planned with the dining room in front and this all works out very nicely.

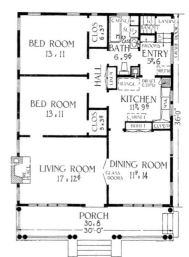

# THE TRUE COST OF BUILDING FROM STILLWELL PLANS

Our estimates of cost may be above or below the cost in any given locality, depending upon the wage scale, prices of material and climatic conditions.

If you were in Los Angeles today, you would know why a home costs much less here than in any Eastern city. Here, and in certain other parts of the country, conditions are favorable for the lowest building costs. However, our *estimates are not local,* they are *relatively correct* and are calculated to be *average* United States costs based on 1919 reports.

Broadly speaking, the cost of building is lowest along the Pacific slope and in what we know as the South from Texas and along the Gulf coast and the south Atlantic coast. It is higher in the Central and New England states and the very highest in Canada, the Intermountain states, the north Central states and in all districts that show great industrial activity. It does no good to speculate or "guesstimate," as some say, on cost—the *only way to find out*

anything dependable about cost is to submit complete detailed plans to builders operating in the given locality. Don't guess or expect anyone else to do so.

The estimates will be too low under certain conditions. They are *relatively correct,* one as compared with another.

The estimates are made upon *average quality* and upon the *exact contents of the plans.* If anyone from necessity or choice makes enlargement of any part of the building or basement, or selects the most expensive materials, it is bound to affect the cost of building. We are honest in our desire to give interested people exact information so far as possible. We know conditions. We are familiar with prices and general requirements throughout North America, but our experience goes to show that there are *often unaccountable differences of cost under seemingly similar conditions.* Therefore, we take this means of explaining why no one but an experienced builder in the locality can be expected to say what a house will cost.

*Note: Blueprints may be purchased without specifications or lists. Specifications and itemized lists refer frequently to the blueprints. See description of contents on page 63. One cannot determine cost by purchase of lists or specifications alone and their use without blueprints would be very unwise and defeat the purpose for which plans are needed. Therefore, specifications and lists may not be purchased unless plans are ordered.*

**SPECIAL OFFER — Note the 10% discount in the special combined offer. Send for the material list as well as blueprints and get SPECIFICATIONS FREE.**

| Plan No. | Estimated Average (U. S.) 1919 Cost (See Explanation on Pages 56 and 57.) | Blue Prints | Specifications | Material List | Special Combined Price for Blue Prints, Specifications and Material Lists | Plan No. | Estimated Average (U. S.) 1919 Cost (See Explanation on Pages 56 and 57.) | Blue Prints | Specifications | Material List | Special Combined Price for Blue Prints Specifications and Material Lists |
|---|---|---|---|---|---|---|---|---|---|---|---|
| W-95 | $3,600 to $4,300 | $20.00 | $3.00 | $6.00 | $26.00 | W-917 | $4,400 to $5,280 | $20.00 | $3.00 | $6.00 | $26.00 |
| W-96 | 4,900 to 5,880 | 25.00 | 3.00 | 7.00 | 32.00 | W-9171 | 3,700 to 4,440 | 17.50 | 3.00 | 6.00 | 24.00 |
| W-97 | 3,865 to 4,600 | 20.00 | 3.00 | 6.00 | 26.00 | W-918 | 3,675 to 4,400 | 17.50 | 3.00 | 6.00 | 24.00 |
| W-98 | 5,000 to 6,000 | 25.00 | 3.00 | 7.00 | 32.00 | W-9181 | 5,600 to 6,700 | 27.50 | 3.00 | 8.00 | 35.00 |
| W-99 | 5,400 to 6,500 | 27.50 | 3.00 | 8.00 | 35.00 | W-919 | 7,700 to 9,240 | 40.00 | 3.00 | 9.00 | 46.00 |
| W-910 | 3,800 to 4,560 | 20.00 | 3.00 | 6.00 | 26.00 | W-9191 | 6,500 to 7,800 | 32.50 | 3.00 | 8.00 | 39.00 |
| W-911 | 4,500 to 5,400 | 22.50 | 3.00 | 6.00 | 28.00 | W-920 | 5,000 to 6,000 | 25.00 | 3.00 | 7.00 | 32.00 |
| W-912 | 6,300 to 7,500 | 27.50 | 3.00 | 8.00 | 35.00 | W-921 | 4,000 to 4,800 | 20.00 | 3.00 | 6.00 | 26.00 |
| W-913 | 6,000 to 7,000 | 27.50 | 3.00 | 8.00 | 35.00 | W-922 | 4,000 to 4,800 | 20.00 | 3.00 | 6.00 | 26.00 |
| W-914 | 5,000 to 6,000 | 25.00 | 3.00 | 7.00 | 32.00 | W-9221 | 5,000 to 6,000 | 25.00 | 3.00 | 7.00 | 32.00 |
| W-915 | 6,000 to 7,000 | 27.50 | 3.00 | 8.00 | 35.00 | W-923 | 5,000 to 6,000 | 25.00 | 3.00 | 7.00 | 32.00 |
| W-916 | 4,600 to 5,520 | 22.50 | 3.00 | 7.00 | 29.00 | W-9231 | 4,500 to 5,400 | 22.50 | 3.00 | 6.00 | 28.00 |
| W-9161 | 5,100 to 6,120 | 25.00 | 3.00 | 7.00 | 32.00 | W-924 | 3,550 to 4,250 | 17.50 | 3.00 | 6.00 | 24.00 |

Furthermore, we never can know what kinds, grades and qualities, catalog numbers, etc., the Owner may fill into the blanks in the specifications provided for the purpose. (See contents of specifications on page 63.) We don't know what per cent. of profit a contractor may need to keep him in business during the idle winter months. In short, we are not mind readers.

We are not prophets or profiteers and it is not necessary for us to list unbelievably low estimates to sell plans. We make the foregoing statement to eliminate unnecessary correspondence.

Any correspondent can, without inconvenience or expense to himself, ascertain what any house will actually cost by sending for the plans on approval as stated in the five offers on page 63. These are the fairest offers made by any architect in the United States. Don't let any local builder estimate from the pictures and sketch plan in the books; that is the merest guessing without any knowledge of the contents of the plans or specifications.

Our estimates include all costs, except the electrical fixtures and the heating plant are not included. These are subject to a greater variation of cost than other selections that the Owner makes and generally are separate contracts. The difference between figures will represent the range of bids one may expect to receive.

To determine the *exact cost*, just request us to submit plans on approval *according to our offers on pages 34 and 63. You will be under no expense or obligation to your contractor or to us.*

*Note: Blueprints may be purchased without specifications or lists. Specifications and itemized lists refer frequently to the blueprints. See description of contents on page 63. One cannot determine cost by purchase of lists or specifications alone and their use without blueprints would be very unwise and defeat the purpose for which plans are needed. Therefore, specifications and lists may not be purchased unless plans are ordered.*

## TAKE ADVANTAGE OF THESE FIVE OFFERS

### YOU WILL NOT BE UNDER ANY OBLIGATION OR EXPENSE IF, AFTER EXAMINATION, YOU CAN NOT USE THE PLANS

**MONEY-BACK OFFER—(1).** Remit with order and we will send plans pre-paid by return mail. If they do not prove to be what you want, return them within 10 days of receipt and we will refund all your money.

**EXPRESS C. O. D. OFFER—(2).** Plans sent C. O. D. with privilege of examination.

**BANK C. O. D. OFFER—(3).** We will consign plans to your bank with special instructions to allow 10-day examination and contractor to figure for cost.

**SPECIAL CONSIGNMENT OFFER—(4).** Plans consigned on approval direct to any firm or individual, but a certified check (which we will hold) must accompany such request as a guarantee that plans will either be paid for or returned within the 10 days allowed for inspection. If we don't hear from you by the expiration of 10 days plus the time required for the transmission of mails, we will then deposit the check.

**EXCHANGE OFFER—(5).** If, within 30 days of the receipt of plans you decide they are not just what you want, you may return them and select any other ready-made plans in exchange.

Or, return them within 30 days and credit for what you have paid will be applied in full upon the cost of special plans.

**NOTE:**—All plans returned under the above offers must be returned in good condition and must not be used or copied. The offers refer only to published and ready-made plans; not to plans made to order.

**SPECIAL OFFER** — Note the 10% discount in the special combined offer. Send for the material list as well as blueprints and get **SPECIFICATIONS FREE.**

| Plan No. | Estimated Average (U. S.) 1919 Cost (See Explanation on Pages 56 and 57.) | Blue Prints | Specifications | Material List | Special Combined Price for Blue Prints, Specifications and Material Lists |
|---|---|---|---|---|---|
| W-9241 | $4,200 to $5,000 | $20.00 | $3.00 | $6.00 | $26.00 |
| W-925 | 4,400 to 5,280 | 22.50 | 3.00 | 6.00 | 28.00 |
| W-926 | 4,700 to 5,600 | 25.00 | 3.00 | 7.00 | 32.00 |
| W-927 | 4,000 to 4,800 | 20.00 | 3.00 | 6.00 | 26.00 |
| W-928 | 5,300 to 6,350 | 27.50 | 3.00 | 8.00 | 35.00 |
| W-929 | 5,000 to 6,000 | 27.50 | 3.00 | 8.00 | 35.00 |
| W-930 | 3,275 to 4,000 | 17.50 | 3.00 | 6.00 | 24.00 |
| W-935 | 3,600 to 4,300 | 20.00 | 3.00 | 6.00 | 26.00 |
| W-936 | 4,000 to 4,800 | 20.00 | 3.00 | 6.00 | 26.00 |

| Plan No. | Estimated Average (U. S.) 1919 Cost (See Explanation on Pages 56 and 57.) | Blue Prints | Specifications | Material List | Special Combined Price for Blue Prints, Specifications and Material Lists |
|---|---|---|---|---|---|
| W-937 | $4,200 to $5,000 | $22.50 | $3.00 | $7.00 | $29.00 |
| W-938 | 4,000 to 4,800 | 20.00 | 3.00 | 6.00 | 26.00 |
| W-939 | 3,900 to 4,680 | 20.00 | 3.00 | 6.00 | 26.00 |
| W-9391 | 4,300 to 5,160 | 22.50 | 3.00 | 6.00 | 28.00 |
| W-940 | 4,600 to 5,500 | 22.50 | 3.00 | 6.00 | 28.00 |
| W-941 | 4,450 to 5,350 | 22.50 | 3.00 | 6.00 | 28.00 |
| W-942 | 5,000 to 6,000 | 25.00 | 3.00 | 7.00 | 32.00 |
| W-943 | 3,800 to 4,550 | 20.00 | 3.00 | 6.00 | 26.00 |
| W-944 | 4,400 to 5,280 | 22.50 | 3.00 | 6.00 | 28.00 |

# GO TO ORIGINAL SOURCES FOR GENUINE BUNGALOW PLANS

Those who are familiar with recent developments in the architecture of modest homes realize that a great change has come about within the past 15 years. The change has been gradual, but is revolutionary as regards external design, interior planning and quality of construction.

California is the home of the Bungalow, so to speak. Climatic and other conditions here are conducive to the development of a home architecture far in advance of the rest of the country. Gradually the ideas originated here have been adopted by homebuilders elsewhere. In other localities certain changes are necessary to meet colder climatic requirements, but these need not alter the true Bungalow style. That which may be necessary for comfort and convenience may possibly change a plan a little, but the genuine California Bungalow Style may be reproduced faithfully, provided suitable plans from original sources are employed.

If, however, the lines of a characteristic California-built Bungalow are altered or "modified" by the average builder, the result usually is a disappointment. In the "modified forms" of the so-called Eastern Bungalows, the style loses much of its identity and characteristic charm. The true bungalow style is simplicity itself and changing the details of a simple design by anyone other than a specialist almost always shows up as freakishness, clumsiness or other obvious incongruity when it is too late to change.

Since 1906, it has been the business of this organization to make plans in the genuine California Bungalow style applicable to varying climatic conditions. The Stillwell plan service passes along these California ideas to other localities, adapting and standardizing the plans of original bungalow homes.

There are not many architects in the country who have specialized on homes sufficiently to make themselves really good designers of such. They have not acquired the speed that will permit them to take work at a price which people can afford to pay.

We serve people everywhere. By specialization and by quantity production, we render superior service at fees so reasonable that it means a real saving in the end. Stillwell plans insure satisfaction during the course of construction and in future years — the cheapest of all insurance.

## Most Bungalows Suitable for Cold Climates

Most of the houses in this book are suitable for building in cold climates. All have brick or concrete foundations. Those floor plans which do not show a stairway leading to a cellar are not originally planned with such and the material lists for these houses do not list double floor or sheathing material. The specifications, however, are made up blank and these things as well as basement construction are mentioned in them and may be filled in or cut out as desired.

For most of the bungalows that do not contemplate a cellar or basement in our original plans, we have extra or supplementary foundation sheets specifying them. We include such plans with our original plans on request. We are also always glad to suggest ways by which some desired re-arrangement may be effected.

| Plan No. | Estimated Average (U. S.) 1919 Cost (See Explanation on Pages 56 and 57.) | Blue Prints | Specifications | Material List | Special Combined Price for Blue Prints, Specifications and Material Lists |
|---|---|---|---|---|---|
| W-9441 | $5,500 to $6,600 | $27.50 | $3.00 | $8.00 | $35.00 |
| W-945 | 5,000 to 6,000 | 27.50 | 3.00 | 8.00 | 35.00 |
| W-946 | 4,000 to 4,800 | 20.00 | 3.00 | 6.00 | 26.00 |
| W-9461 | 4,600 to 5,500 | 22.50 | 3.00 | 7.00 | 29.00 |
| W-947 | 4,500 to 5,300 | 22.50 | 3.00 | 6.00 | 28.00 |
| W-948 | 5,000 to 6,000 | 25.00 | 3.00 | 7.00 | 32.00 |
| W-949 | 5,500 to 6,600 | 27.50 | 3.00 | 8.00 | 35.00 |
| W-950 | 5,500 to 6,600 | 30.00 | 3.00 | 8.00 | 37.00 |
| W-951 | 3,850 to 4,600 | 20.00 | 3.00 | 6.00 | 26.00 |
| W-952 | 2,650 to 3,180 | 15.00 | 3.00 | 5.00 | 21.00 |
| W-9521 | 3,150 to 3,700 | 17.50 | 3.00 | 6.00 | 24.00 |

| Plan No. | Estimated Average (U. S.) 1919 Cost (See Explanation on Pages 56 and 57.) | Blue Prints | Specifications | Material List | Special Combined Price for Blue Prints, Specifications and Material Lists |
|---|---|---|---|---|---|
| W-953 | $4,200 to $5,000 | $25.00 | $3.00 | $6.00 | $31.00 |
| W-9531 | 4,675 to 5,600 | 25.00 | 3.00 | 6.00 | 31.00 |
| W-954 | 4,500 to 5,400 | 22.50 | 3.00 | 7.00 | 29.00 |
| W-9541 | 3,800 to 4,550 | 22.50 | 3.00 | 7.00 | 29.00 |
| W-955 | 4,500 to 5,400 | 22.50 | 3.00 | 7.00 | 29.00 |
| W-9551 | 4,500 to 5,400 | 22.50 | 3.00 | 7.00 | 29.00 |
| W-959 | 3,000 to 3,500 | 15.00 | 3.00 | 5.00 | 21.00 |
| W-9591 | 3,000 to 3,500 | 15.00 | 3.00 | 5.00 | 21.00 |
| W-960 | 4,300 to 5,100 | 20.00 | 3.00 | 6.00 | 26.00 |
| W-9601 | 3,500 to 4,200 | 20.00 | 3.00 | 6.00 | 26.00 |
| | | | | | |

### No. W-959

Always, the problem is, how to get much house in a small space. This square shape is one solution. The house has a good brick foundation but no cellar. Siding walls with shingled roof and front porch gable. While the width of the dining room is very little, the colonade in reality overcomes any appearance of smallness in the interior.

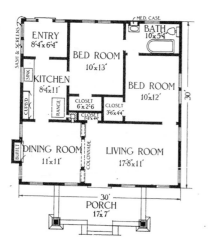

### No. W-9591

This is another big-looking Bungalow that can be built at comparatively low cost. There is a good foundation but no cellar, although that could easily be arranged with inside stairs off the enclosed kitchen porch. The absence of any interior pass hall leaves large closets and the bed rooms open conveniently into the bath room.

## No. W-960

This Bungalow is 40x26 feet. The exterior is stained siding with painted trimmings. The porch is cobble-stones and cement. The roof shingles.

This shows what a striking appearance a small inexpensive house may have.

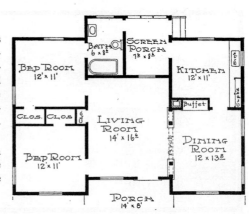

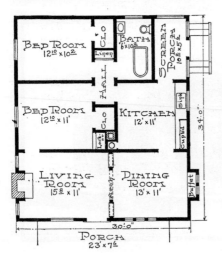

## No. W-9601

This home has a brick and cement porch, sided walls and shingle roof. There is no cellar, although one may be arranged for with inside stairs from the enclosed porch.

This is the most compact plan it is possible to arrange with the two principal rooms in front.

## REVERSING PLANS

*Plans will be sent reversed to suit location or frontage.* There is no extra charge for reversing.

## CHANGES IN PLANS

We will gladly advise in the matter of changes. Arrange minor changes with your local builder by marking up the plans after you get them, or by stipulating the changes in the contract.

Regarding the specification of one kind of material instead of another, see description of specifications on page 63. Note that, while plans may show a house with walls of siding, the blanks in the specifications are arranged in such a way that shingles or stucco may be written in. Similarly, other selections may be made. That is one of the advantages of using standardized plans.

If you want to save money by using ready-made plans, but still wish to have alteration drawings made to indicate minor changes in the floor plan or in the exterior or both, then take advantage of one of our special sketch offers on page 62. Just send for the stock plans at listed prices plus the additional amount for alteration sketches as explained in the Sketch Offers on the next page.

Our blueprint plans are made from master drawings or negatives that can not be altered. Changes that do not require a complete set of new drawings can most cheaply be arranged as described above and this method is generally very satisfactory.

For changes that require complete revision and an entire new set of drawings, our charges are about double the price of ready-made plans.

# Compare the Value of Plans with Rent, Taxes and Insurance

¶ The price of a set of Stillwell ready-made plans is less than one month's rent for a house.

¶ Plans cost less than one year's taxes.

¶ If you divide the cost of plans by only ten years of the life of the building, they are cheaper than fire insurance.

¶ Unlike rent, taxes and insurance, plans are paid for but once while the beneficial results are permanent.

¶ *Stillwell Plans give by far the greatest return, dollar for dollar, of any expenditure for the home.*

# PLANS MADE TO ORDER

While many people find our ready-prepared plans entirely satisfactory and can readily make suitable selections (arranging any minor changes with the builders), others are unable to find what they need. We cannot hope to carry a stock of plans that will meet everybody's requirements, but we are prepared to draw special plans to order. We will draw plans for any size of house and design the exterior in any style of architecture — English — French — Italian — Spanish — or any other.

If you wish to see how your ideas actually work out, and would like to have them outlined in such a form that your local builders can use them to give you an approximate estimate of cost to build, then take advantage of our Special Sketch Offers. You will be under no further obligations for expense if you do not want detailed working plans completed.

The first step is very simple and will help to clarify your own ideas. Make a brief outline of your essential requirements, send sketches of floor plans and clippings of special features. If you have no accurate floor plan, please try to make just a rough outline, using the sketch pages in the front of the book and making each small square equal one foot. Then fill out the questionnaire, in the back of the book. With this information, which any one can furnish, we will serve you virtually as well as if the work were directed by personal interviews.

# SPECIAL SKETCH OFFER

**FOR FLOOR PLANS ONLY:**

**Sketch Offer No. 1**

Our charge is 50 cents for each principal room, each bath, each front and side porch, and each large hall.

We will draw floor plans to the regular working plan scale of one-fourth inch equals one foot, making plans which are four or five times wider and longer than those in this book.

**Sketch Offer No. 2**

If you want floor plans and also the front elevation and one side elevation to show the outside appearance of the house, figure the cost at $1.50 for each principal room, front and side porch, and each large hall.

**Example No. 1**

Under Sketch Offer No. 1, a floor plan similar to No. W-98 will cost $3.50.

Under Sketch Offer No. 2, a plan with two elevations will cost $10.50.

**Example No. 2**

As Applied to Plan No. W-915.
Proposition No. 1, Cost.....................$ 4.50
Proposition No. 2, Cost......................13.50

NOTE: These sketch propositions are an entirely unprofitable phase of our work, but it is hoped they will finally lead to orders for detailed working plans.

Being unprofitable, it is expected that remittances will accompany all orders for sketches.

## FIVE SPECIAL OFFERS OF PLANS ON APPROVAL

The purpose of these offers is:

**First**—To enable anyone to get plans and figure cost of building before finally deciding to keep them.

**Second**—To give correspondents a chance to see what each house actually looks like from all sides.

**Third**—To guarantee prospective purchasers that the plans are what they need, that they are complete as represented and worth the price. This is very important as there are a large number of inferior plans on the market, and prices of plans mean absolutely nothing as regards quality of draftsmanship from various sources.

## GUARANTEED MONEY-BACK, EXCHANGE, C. O. D. AND PLANS-ON-APPROVAL OFFERS

**MONEY-BACK OFFER**—Remit with order and we will send plans prepaid by return mail. If they do not prove to be what you want, return them within 10 days of receipt and we will refund your money.

**EXPRESS C. O. D. OFFER**—Plans sent C. O. D. with privilege of examination.

(The U. S. Parcel Post will not carry plans and specifications C. O. D.)

**BANK C. O. D. OFFER**—We will consign plans to your bank with special instructions to allow 10-day examination and contractor to figure for cost.

**SPECIAL CONSIGNMENT OFFER**—Plans consigned on approval direct to any firm or individual, but a certified check (which we will hold), must accompany such request as a guarantee that plans will either be paid for or returned within a 10-day limit allowed for inspection. If we don't hear from you by the expiration of 10 days plus the time required for the transmission of mails, we will then deposit the check. Should you not want to keep the plans and send them back within the 10-day limit, we will return the check.

**EXCHANGE OFFER**—If, within 30 days of the receipt of plans, you decide they are not just what you want, you may return them and select any other ready-made plans in exchange.

Or, return them within 30 days and credit for what you have paid will be applied in full upon the cost of special plans.

**NOTE**—All plans returned under the above offers must be returned in good condition and must not be used or copied, or notes marked on them.

**REMITTANCE REQUIRED**—A remittance must accompany all orders, from firms as well as individuals. Otherwise plans will be sent C. O. D. regardless of references or financial ratings. In this way service is economized and prices to all purchasers are kept at the lowest possible point by the elimination of unnecessary correspondence and the keeping of accounts.

## CONTENTS OF STILLWELL PLANS

(1) **General Plans** consist of Foundation Plan, Floor Plans and Four Elevations, all drawn to a scale of ¼ inch equals one foot. Foundation plans having basements are planned for the location of the heating plant, etc. We do not specify the kind of heating nor the various pipes and outlets, since there are so many different systems and climatic requirements.

All dimensions of all plans are carefully figured. Everything is plain and simple, all the work being prepared in such a way that any ordinary contractor can duplicate the houses anywhere to the entire satisfaction of the Owner.

Plans show the sizes and locations of all doors, windows, lights, switches, plumbing fixtures, etc., etc. Elevations show the front and rear and side views, specifying only that which cannot be so well specified elsewhere.

(2) **Detail Drawings** are equal in importance to the General Plans and are specially featured in all Stillwell plans. Knowing that our plans leave our personal supervision, we prepare our detail drawings with greater care and make them more complete than architects usually do. This applies to foundation and framing sections, fireplaces, interior finish and cabinet work, such as bookcases, seats, cupboards of all kinds, buffet, stairway, etc., etc. Most of these details are drawn to a scale of ¾ inch equals one foot and have sectional drawings as well as front views.

(3) **Specifications** explain the general conditions of the contract. They cover all phases of the work—excavations, concrete, masonry, rough and finish carpenter work, plastering, plumbing, hardware, wiring, painting, etc.

These specifications are a very long, standardized, mimeographed form with a large number of blank spaces for the filling in of the Owner's selections. This makes it easy for the Owner to control the cost and to select what his local market affords, conferring, of course, with the local contractors and material men. These specifications, together with blueprints are the vital part—the sum and substance—the basis of the contract, without which building is a wasteful gamble.

(4) **Itemized Material Lists.** Every lumber dealer knows that one of the great defects of the present methods of contracting is the inability of the average contractor to make out a correct material list. He hasn't the time nor the patience to list all the small items with care and something is always overlooked. This is bad for the contractor as well as the Owner, as there is always a big "extra" list. Without correct material lists it is impossible to know what a finished house is going to cost.

Our lists are prepared by practical estimators and are really complete. Everything is itemized and segregated in such a way as to make verification by the Contractor easy. Likewise he can add to or deduct quantities, according to changes that may be desired.

## FINE LOOKING

I have just finished a Bungalow for Mr. M. E. Converse from your plans. It is a fine looking building.

FRANK S. CHENEY,
Builder and Contractor.

Winchendon, Massachusetts.

## CONTRACTOR GIVES SOUND ADVICE

. . . Now I have a personal friend who is a good carpenter and contractor, whom I will want to handle the whole job for me. Of course he could draw his own plans, but I have shown him your books and he has advised me to get your plans, as they would probably be more complete than he would care to make. He has known of your Company for a number of years, and thinks highly of your plans.

G. A. DUNCAN.

Bellingham, Washington.

## ATTORNEY RECOGNIZES VALUE OF PLANS

Enclosed please find check for duplicate plans of your No. ——.
Will say that plans and material list are thoroughly satisfactory, and contractor claims they are better than some of the plans furnished in Fort Wayne, and compare very favorably with work of Chicago and New York architects.

O. E. FUELBER,
Attorney.

Fort Wayne, Indiana.

## MILL MEN ADVISE COMPLETE PLANS

Enclosed find check for which send me plans and specifications of the Bungalow ——. I am a carpenter and mill man of several years experience and am getting these plans for people who are going to build. . . . They think to build a good home that it is not necessary to have plans, but I have explained that it would be more satisfactory to both parties, contractor and owner, as they want to contract the job.

R. O. CASSITY,
Builder.

Ingomar, California.

## PLANS FOR CONTRACTOR'S OWN HOME

The plans arrived in due time and I am well pleased with them. I will be glad to send you a picture of the house when it is completed.

L. L. CARMAN,
Contractor and Builder.

Sayre, Pa.

## NEVER WORKED WITH BETTER PLANS

I have my house nearly completed according to plans and specifications furnished by you. . . . I am very much pleased with the house and the contractor says he never worked with better plans. . . . Everything is entirely satisfactory.

W. E. PHELPS.

Garland, Utah.

## BEST READY-MADE PLANS EVER USED

We are building Bungalow No. —— according to plans purchased of you some time ago. I would appreciate very much advice from you as to the most attractive scheme of outside painting. . . . One builder was very much taken with your plans, saying they were the best ready-made plans he had ever used.

MRS. KARL D. BICKEL.

McGregor, Iowa.

## BUILDERS LIKE TO USE GOOD PLANS

I used your plan sent to me. I like it very much and now am sending for more.

S. W. BLIVEN,
Contractor and Builder.

Dyersburg, Tennessee.

## PLEASED AND NO CHANGES REQUIRED

I have just completed a Bungalow for Mr. E. A. Dye, built from your plan ——, and it is said by everybody to be the finest building in town. No changes were made except to put window sash in the screen porch to match the balance of the house.

L. L. RUNDLE,
Contractor and Builder.

Logan, Kansas.

## PLANS COMPLETE

The plans and specifications which you sent me through the First National Bank here were received and have given them careful consideration. . . . The completeness with which these plans have been gotten out is worthy of congratulation.

H. M. SEAGERS,
Corona Typewriter Company, Inc.

Groton, New York.

## EXPERIENCED BUILDERS USE PLANS

We are extensive bungalow builders, and greatly interested in your designs and plans. Enclosed please find order for two sets of plans for Bungalows, and check covering cost of same.

FOREST PARK IMPROVEMENT CO.

New York City.

## SATISFACTORY AFTER TEST OF YEARS

Several years ago I purchased two sets of plans from you, and the houses proved very satisfactory. I am planning on building another house here and ask . . . that you send plan No. ——, in your West Coast Bungalows.

W. R. KRAPFEL,
Builder.

Centerville, Iowa.

## CONTRACTORS WELL PLEASED

We find that in the erection of the Little Bungalow —— we are in need of a duplicate set of plans, and are enclosing check for same. We are well pleased with the original plan.

FOWLER BROTHERS.

Riverdale, California.

## WORTH TWICE ORDINARY ARCHITECT'S PLANS

. . . In regard to your plans of houses and Bungalows, I honestly believe they are worth twice (if not more) than what one pays an architect for. They are all clear, so any one can understand them.

L. J. EASTERBROOK,
Lumber, Lath, Roofing, Cement.

Saybrook, Illinois.

## CONTRACTOR PLEASED WITH HIS OWN HOME

. . . I have a good photo of my home which I built from your plans. Shall be glad to send it to you if you care for same.

S. S. PALMA,
Contractor.

Lafayette, Indiana.

## PLANS GOOD FOR THE SOUTH

I used one of your plans last summer in building a Bungalow and I like it very well. I expect to build three or four houses this year and will probably get all the plans from you.

C. C. BELL.

West Monroe, Louisiana.

## THE SECOND BUNGALOW

. . . This will make the second Bungalow I have built by your plans. The first turned out most satisfactorily.

FREDERICK M. JOHNSON.

Napa, California.

## CLIENT WELL PLEASED

Beg to say that the plans for the Bungalow were received by express today and my client seems to be very well pleased with same.

ALFRED G. PAGE,
Contractor and Builder.

Elizabeth City, North Carolina.

## HAS BUILT SEVERAL WHICH SOLD WELL

I have built from the plan which I recently purchased from you, which has turned out very satisfactorily, and I now write for information in regard to others.

SIDNEY RANKIN.

Olympia, Washington.